# THE EFFECTS OF THE DIGITAL MARKETING ECOSYSTEM ON THE GLOBAL REAL ESTATE MARKET

BY:

WELLINGTON KIIRU

Copyright © 2019 by wellington kiiru

All rights reserved. No part of this book may be used or reproduced by any means, graphic, electronic, or mechanical, including photocopying, recording, taping, or by any information storage retrieval system, without the written permission of the publisher except in the case of brief quotations embodied in critical articles and reviews.

# Table of Contents

INTRODUCTION: ........................................................................... 1

HOW DIGITAL MARKETING WILL CHANGE THE REAL ESTATE MARKET IN 2019 ............................................................ 8

REAL ESTATE DIGITAL MARKETING TECHNIQUES THAT WORK WONDERS ................................................................. 14

CASE STUDY: Digital Marketing for a leading real estate developer in Chennai ................................................................. 26

# INTRODUCTION:

Marketing for any product or service digitally has now become mandatory. With over 234 million internet users currently, the digital market has really opened up a plethora of opportunities for brands today. Real estate is one such industry that has really benefitted from the digital marketing wave. According to research, around 92% of potential buyers do vigorous research online before they ultimately make the purchase offline. Hence, making sure you have a strong Digital Marketing Strategy is of the utmost importance to make your brand name stand out in the real estate industry.

So, what makes Digital Marketing For Real Estate such a vital tool for developers and home seekers?

Technology continues to be a catalyst for change in all areas of business and industry, and the real estate market is no exception (Behl, 2016). Today's worker is more mobile and more connected than ever before, which means that businesses can operate anywhere. Especially in mature urban centres, the pushback against escalating real estate leasing and ownership costs is escalating.

Digital Marketing has revolutionized real estate industry in a significant way.

The industry of real estate in India has matured enough where buyers are doing extensive research online before actually making their final purchase (Behl, 2016). The buyers in the market are searching for the brokers, dealers, projects, and sellers online, which make the digital marketing even more lucrative for real estate industry.

While telecommuting may not be a viable option for all companies, or even all employees within a company, many organizations have utilized remote work models with great success (Behl, 2016). This is reducing the amount of office space needed to accommodate employees, and it is changing the dynamics of what constitutes a ideal - read expensive - location.

The distributed work model itself is not new. Health insurer Aetna has used remote work as an employee retention tool for more than 20 years, and more than 31% of the company's employees telework (Behl, 2016). Through telecommuting, the company has reduced its office space by more than 2 million square feet, resulting in an approximate annual savings of $78 million. The company also closed and demolished its 1.3 million Square foot building in Middletown, Connecticut, which was praised as the "office park of the future" when it was built in the 1980s.

So why all the buzz now? These are just a few ways technology-focused factors:

- Innovations in cloud-based information storage security
- Improved functionality of enterprise software such as Microsoft SharePoint and OneDrive
- Rising reliability of communications applications such as Skype and GoToMeeting
- Greater coverage and relative decreases in the costs of wifi, cellular, and high-speed internet access
- Online marketplaces such as Behance, Fiverr, Upwork, and hundreds of others facilitating connections between workers and employers around the world
- Working in concert with one another, the convergence of these factors and the ever-present pressure for companies to streamline costs, is making remote work viable for a wider array of knowledge workers than ever before. According to FlexJobs.com, 2014 saw a 26% increase in remote job postings over 2013. This directly translates to smaller footprints of traditional office space that companies need to lease, purchase, or build.

While companies like Aetna have made telecommuting a part of the company culture, other companies, like Yahoo! Have shifted away from home-based work, bringing their employees back together. In 2013, when the company announced it would be ending work-at-home opportunities, then head of Human Resources, Jackie Reses said, "Some of the best decisions and insights come from hallway and cafeteria discussions, meeting new people, and impromptu team meetings."

Therefore, companies are looking to innovative, flexible, and adaptable office designs to help inspire and facilitate these impromptu team meetings. Instead of floors full of cubicles, which often sit empty while meeting spaces are overbooked, shared workspaces, meeting spaces, social areas abound - often enabled with video conferencing, smartboards, and other virtual

Collaboration technologies (Behl, 2016). When GlaxoSmithKline relocated from their former location in a leased office space in downtown Philadelphia to the historic Navy Yard, The Company used the principles of communities to create an open, vibrant and collaborative work experience.

As a result, it was able to relocate the entire population of 1,300 employees from their former location in downtown Philadelphia while reducing their office space by 600,000 square feet (KPMG International, 2018). While the services provided have had numerous benefits for GlaxoSmithKline's bottom line, the move also spiked the percentage of unleased space in the Philadelphia urban core.

Collaborative workplace organizations, such as WeWork and Workspring, are also knocking down the literal and figurative "walls" and changing commercial real estate dynamics. These shared office spaces provide various options for companies that either lack the capital or want to divest themselves of the real estate, furniture, services, etc (KPMG International, 2018). That were previously non-negotiable. These shared spaces are ideal for hosting meetings, as well as for both on-demand and long-term space for satellite employees, mobile workers, and independent professionals.

In addition to reducing the amount of office space a company needs, and re-imagining how that space is used, technology is also bringing down barriers between potential tenants and real estate owners. Developments in cloud computing combined with mobile and social media are resulting in cost-effective and real-time property information, which means many leasing activities are happening online.

As technology continues to develop and these trends gain more traction in the market, I foresee the following developments:

- In the most mature real estate markets, such as New York or London, rents may have peaked (KPMG International, 2018). Landlords are already reducing rates to attract tenants to Midtown Manhattan, for instance, in reaction to migrations prompted by untenable real estate costs.
- Co-location and space sharing will increase for smaller companies, and shared services across companies could become the norm.
- "Location, location, location" will remain a key factor for several sectors that rely on talent, transportation, and ease of access to other companies. Businesses with distributed real estate models will reduce their assets to token Sales Office presences in the metropolitan

**areas.**

- Because technology is ever-changing, the challenge for traditional commercial office environments - to keep pace with cabling, power, and other infrastructure requirements - will continue.
- With further consolidation of real estate data on the web and the rise of smart buildings, the role of broker will change to advisor. More and more owners will embrace online

services for engaging tenants, sidestepping brokerage fees - similar to the way Airbnb is transforming the hospitality market. This only stands to increase transparency and serve the tenant's interests, both by exposing them to a wider array of properties and by making it easier to cost-compare.

- Social amenities of urban center will continue to draw young talent willing to sacrifice living space - even opting for dormitory-style apartment sharing. The live/work space in the Brooklyn Navy Yards is just one example (Douglas, 2018). As millennials establish families or desire more space, less congestion, and different community features, retreat to suburban and exurban homes will not limit professional options as greatly as in the past - I predict that companies that telework will outpace those who are reining it in.

- The work-life divide has been blurred for at least a generation. Ease of communication and access has distorted what were once "normal business hours" to the point that employers are recognizing the counter intuitively negative effect on productivity (Douglas, 2018). In response, forward-thinking companies are instituting "Work Free" hours and mandating that employees switch off work devices at home. Once the "Work-Life Merger" cultural phenomenon finds its equilibrium, the need for separate social spaces vs. office spaces will increase.

# HOW DIGITAL MARKETING WILL CHANGE THE REAL ESTATE MARKET IN 2019

**Boost Exposure**

Numerous commercial projects vary in size, cost, and location. With that in mind, digital presence becomes a vital task.

To stay on par with the changing scene, electronic marketers require remaining in line with the progressing technology patterns.

When you use social media marketing, for example, you need to relentlessly conduct research about your customers to know what makes them involved with brands.

**Digital Marketing Automation**

As a landlord, for example, there is not enough time for you to perform digital marketing on your own. Digital marketing requires you to be more engaging, develop more content and do more customization (Douglas, 2018).

But time is insufficient for your case. However, you can utilize the time you have in a more efficient way. For that reason, digital marketing for landlords automation platforms are valuable for your situation (Douglas, 2018).

Through right setup, it is possible to automate your many marketing jobs, like running email campaigns, delivering targeted pieces, etc. The good news is that these tools are more affordable in 2019 (Douglas, 2018).

## Chatbots

These tools have been around for a long time. The technology incorporates voice, text, and messages to talk straight with customers (Douglas, 2018). Chatbots are utilized much longer than virtual reality. However, it is taking the spotlight now and in the coming years.

The market of chatbot of chatbot would have an annual growth rate of more than 24%. It expected to reach $1.25 billion a few years from now. The majority of businesses now are using chatbots as part of their customer support (Douglas, 2018).

In fact, several messaging apps are using bots to promote products and services. The apps offer chatbots to help brands in promoting their products and services while providing a personalized customer support experience.

It is a successful technology because it can quickly and accurately provide answers to the

client's questions. Furthermore, they can gather data about their users. These data are effective in boosting interaction with them.

Chatbots offer a more responsive way in dealing with customers.

**Augmented Reality**

The greatest challenge with real estate marketing is that clients need to see the property in person before they make a final choice. The good thing is that you can add augmented reality to your digital marketing (Douglas, 2018).

There are several tools that let you produce virtual tours of properties. They can present to your clients what a certain construction project will appear when it is finished.

Virtual tours of the neighbourhood are now deemed necessary.

The reason for this is that tours could give your clients a feel for the surrounding area. They enable them to comprehend how it would feel like if they live in the property and the neighbourhood.

Technology firms are also releasing toolkits that make augmented offerings a lot easier. In this case, augmented technology becomes more accessible in 2019 (Raman, 2019).

## Blockchain Technology

Blockchain technology is currently disrupting how the globe views financing and monetary systems. Rentberry, for example, is a rental platform that utilizes this technology to simplify the rental process for tenants and renters (Raman, 2019). But the advantages of this technology are now being utilized in digital marketing as well.

This technology enables marketers in tracking their ads placement and ensuring their consumers that they click their ads. As an result, customer engagement data become more accurate and relabel (Raman, 2019). That said, your marketing assets will not be wasted.

With its transparent nature, it gives consumers more control over what and how their personal information is being used by marketers. When they trust you, they are likely to share their personal data. It helps you know more about them better.

## Social Ad Campaigns

Social media is a reliable marketing channel. Several companies still do not totally comprehend how extremely effective these systems have ended up being (Raman, 2019).

A variety of fresh offers from the huge networks made it possible to get to target markets specifically and more effectively than in the past (Raman, 2019). These fresh offers would include geofencing and improved retargeting.

The trick to maximizing it is to create advanced social projects that utilize the complete variety of tools and styles (Raman, 2019). Companies that invest in advanced social methods are most likely to find an outstanding ROI on their investment.

**Influencer Marketing**

Another major trend which is coming up in real estate business is the use of social media influencers to create a buzz for the upcoming projects. These influencers are not celebrities and big personalities but general public who have huge number of follower base in social media channels (Raman, 2019). Thus influencers are not highly paid brand ambassadors but instead a public figure whose opinions can influence customer buying behavior which is a much cheaper option for real estate clients. Social Beat has a product called influencer

(Raman, 2019).in where a large number of influencers sign up. These influencers are outsourced to clients to write blogs for their projects and also post backlinks on their social media profiles.

People want authentic and real experiences. That's why your potential clients are likely to believe an real person over the ad that you show. And this is where influencer marketing becomes useful. It is costly. But it is also effective.

If you use it in your real estate marketing, you need to find influencers that can reach out to your right consumers (Raman, 2019). To further assist your campaign, you can use an effective hashtag that your clients can remember easily.

# REAL ESTATE DIGITAL MARKETING TECHNIQUES THAT WORK WONDERS

For any real estate developer who is hoping to succeed, digital marketing is a great place to start. Developers not using this medium are losing out a plethora of opportunities that the medium has to offer (Golden, 2018). Here are some of the strategies that a developer can use:

Building a strong real estate brand through a website, social media marketing, content marketing and search engine optimisation

Acquiring customers through advertising on various platforms such as Facebook, Google, LinkedIn, lead nurturing techniques and influencer marketing

Customer engagement via YouTube videos and social media posts

Let's look at some digital marketing practices (in the Real Estate Industry) that will help achieve the above-mentioned goals.

## 1. Building the brand

Creating an online presence is the first, most important step, and serves as a backbone for all future digital marketing activities. To establish a powerful online presence, Real Estate developers need to focus on creating three things.

## Creating a Website

For Real Estate, a website can serve two purposes: a virtual office that showcases the builder's latest projects or a virtual marketplace for home seekers to explore purchasing options (Golden, 2018). To make either one or both of these purposes work well, there are Numerous Tools and Optimisation Techniques That Need To Be Implemented.

Even the Design of the Website matters as it can make a difference to user experience and one such design that has been making wave's amongst the real estate websites is an Flat Design (Golden, 2018). Flat website designs are categorised by their simple, elegant and square'ish' look; first noticed in the Windows 8 Tile User Interface. With minimalistic animations and loads of white space, the Flat website design has proven to be effective in page speed loading times, readability, mobile optimisation and ease of navigation.

While a good website design is pleasing to the eyes, it only scratches the surface of what matters especially in the Real Estate sector. A stellar design needs to be accompanied with great content to create an impact. Writing Good Content that effectively communicates a Real Estate brand's message and intrigues the user to go ahead for a purchase is vital. Presenting Your Target Audience With Engaging Content is a sure-shot way to grab their attention and generate leads.

Real Estate is a very broad topic, so to fit everything into a single website, other strategies can be utilised to showcase everything a Real Estate developer has to offer.

Multiple Web pages: Aside from having a homepage that gives a gist of the Real Estate builder's brand, having multiple web pages that provide more information on the brand and interlink with one another through clever content navigation is essential (Golden, 2018). More pages ultimately result in users spending more time on the website, which directly affects the website's rank on search engines.

Landing Pages: Landing Pages act as mini e-commerce portals that explain in detail about a particular brand's upcoming, on-going or released Real Estate project (LEE, 2018). Landing pages that are interactive or those that have video presentations have proven to yield 403% more inquiries than regular pages.

## Search Engine Optimisation (SEO)

SEO is the glue that holds an entire digital marketing campaign together. As a matter of fact, digital marketers for Real Estate must have an SEO Planner right at the beginning of their marketing strategy (LEE, 2018). From SEO Plugins to various Link Building Techniques, the driving force of good SEO, especially for Real Estate, is keyword research.

Statistics show that 80% of home buyers search for properties online which means having a list of search keywords incorporated into a content marketing strategy will pay off well (LEE, 2018). Potential customers will most likely be presented with search results about a property that has those keywords. Additionally, real estate companies can also Leverage Local SEO And Google Maps To Promote Their Business.

## Creating a Blog

When people need help or are looking for something, they do one of two things – seek out a person or a place or browse the internet. Blogging has come a long way from being a

casual online tool for storytelling to an essential element of a digital marketing strategy.

Blogs are a long, short or creative source of information and if there is one thing Google loves, it is loads of valuable information. Research shows that websites with blogs have 434% more indexed pages (LEE, 2018). Google recognises and ranks these websites easily due to the information provided, ultimately leading to that site showing up on the first page of search results.

Considering how broad a topic Real Estate is, builders must take advantage of the power of blogging and focus on sharing information to potential home buyers. Blogs that give detailed information on upcoming properties, tips on home buying and guides on investment options are just some of the many topics a Real Estate blog can include (LEE, 2018).

**Having a strong social media presence**

The platform of Social Media offers brands a unique way to get more personal with their audience, and it is no different in the case of Real Estate.

**Casa-Grande-fb**

There are numerous platforms for Social Media Marketing available today and some of the most useful ones for Real Estate developers include:

Facebook: India has the world's largest number of Facebook users (195v million and counting), so there is a clear and open platform for Real Estate developers to take advantage of the Numerous Advertising Techniques Facebook Has To Offer.

YouTube: Videos are, without a doubt, the most watched medium on the planet (Osumare, 2018). Real Estate developers can use Optimised YouTube Videos to add a layer of instructiveness to their promotional campaigns.

Twitter: This micro-blogging giant has proven to be a rather useful marketing tool in the recent years. Twitter serves as a great platform for Real Estate developers to invite credible 3rd party sources to influence purchase decisions. For more insight on this, make sure you check out our extensive Twitter Marketing Guide For Businesses In India.

LinkedIn: LinkedIn is the go-to medium for anyone looking to Expand Their Business To Business Portfolio. Real Estate developers can connect to 3rd party realtors, architects, interior designers, house maintenance providers and so on.

## 2. Acquiring Customers

Having an online presence won't be fruitful if your potential customers are not aware of that presence. Real Estate developers depend heavily on lead generation, and digital marketing offers the quickest, easiest and most ROI Friendly Lead Generation Method (Osumare, 2018). Here are some of the ways Real Estate developers can acquire customers via digital media.

## Advertising

Advertising online is one of the best ways to ensure you are reaching your potential target Group. If done right, it can be the best lead generation tool for real estate developers (Osumare, 2018). Be it Facebook or Google or even other platforms such as Bing and Yahoo, using lead generation, website conversion ads or even interactive ads to engage with your target audience and collect leads.

## Facebook Ads

As of July 2017, there are 241 million active users in India on Facebook. This is a primary reason why advertising on Facebook is something every builder needs to try. From website conversion ads to lead ads and carousel ads, builders should try a combination of videos and images to drive enquiries and site visits (Osumare, 2018). Facebook also has detailed targeting by demographics, age and behaviour. Additionally, you can also target your website visitors and those you have engaged with your post so that the ad is displayed to a more specific and niche crowd making the probability of selling the property even higher than before.

Ads in regional languages have started rolling out, and marketers have begun incorporating this concept into their marketing strategies to reach out to their target audience (Osumare, 2018). When a potential home buyer reads an ad in his regional language, he develops a bond of trust and comfort with the seller and is more likely to make a purchase, or at least recommend that product to a friend.

**Regional ads**

With Facebook's Brand Reach and Frequency campaigns, brands can even get assured visibility and reach, similar to what a front-page newspaper ad gives.

**Google Ads**

Google AdWords is a paid digital marketing strategy that is run on the Google search engine. Adwords Smart Display Campaigns run strongly through a set of rules and guidelines and work best when incorporated into SEO tools and strategies.

Let's say a home seeker is typing "flats in OMR" in the search box; if the digital marketer has incorporated the keywords "flats in OMR" along with some other relevant search queries, Google will pick up that ad and display it in the search results (Osumare, 2018). The placement of the ad depends entirely on the budget set for the campaign. You can also Optimise Your AdWords Campaign for profound results.

Google's algorithms are ever changing and evolving to be more consumer-friendly, and 2017 Has Some Cool New Digital Marketing Trends that every marketer must keep close tabs on.

**Drip email marketing**

Drip emails are automated emails that are sent out based on a predefined time or user actions. Real Estate developers can target and constantly stay in touch with a group of people based on certain criteria retrieved from a

Strong Email Marketing Database. Let's say that a customer has visited a property website and shown interest by subscribing to property newsletters (Osumare, 2018). Digital marketers can use the information provided by the customer to send emails about the development and completion of the property and news on various other related properties.

Drip emails are a powerful lead nurturer, with statistics showing a 119% increase click-through rate via trustworthy emails.

## Influencer marketing

Influencer Marketing is the Internet's word-of-mouth marketing method and can prove very effective to generate leads for Real Estate Developers (Osumare, 2018). Just like word-of-mouth, influencer marketing uses popular bloggers and other professionals in the Real Estate industry to promote a particular property. Influencer marketing channels include both blogs and social media channels, so Real estate developers must carefully choose the appropriate kind of influencer to market their properties.

Influencer provides a one-stop platform for Real Estate developers to search and connect with the best influencers in the country; they can choose from either working on long campaigns with a selected influencer or contacting multiple micro-influencers over various social media platforms to spread the word.

## 3. Customer Engagement

The age-old marketing rule of getting new customers while retaining existing customers applies in the digital space as well. Of course, the most popular tool for customer engagement today is social media, and Facebook ranks high up on the list, especially for the Real Estate industry (Osumare, 2018). There are a plethora of Social Media Trends Benefiting The Real Estate Industry. Here are some interesting ways developers can utilise Facebook and YouTube for customer engagement.

### Facebook engagement

- Post real estate investment advice albeit with a funny picture.
- Post product comparison images and let the followers vote.
- Post interesting facts about the locality where the property is being developed.
- Post about celebrity or high-profile activity that is happening in the locality where the property is being developed.
- Post about festivals and celebratory occasions while adding a twist that relates to a property.
- Share information about daily real estate activities.

## YouTube engagement

- Post videos on property interiors
- DIY practical tips on home improvement
- Property reviews
- Live feed of upcoming events that relate to the property
- Virtual reality property experience

# CASE STUDY: Digital Marketing for a leading real estate developer in Chennai

A Chennai based Real Estate enterprise which laid its foundations in 2004 (Osumare, 2018). Known for providing niche residential segments like luxury villas and high-rise apartments, the company has since produced 68 projects, selling to over 4000 happy residents.

They wanted to scale up their digital presence through powerful digital marketing, focusing on five primary goals.

- Improved UX Design
- SEO
- SMM
- Influencer Marketing
- Digital Advertising

An intense digital marketing campaign followed, running on platforms like Facebook, LinkedIn and Google search, resulting in an impressive turnaround that showed:

- Over 500 Crores in sales from digital

**enquiries**

- 10x increase in lead generation
- Cost per lead reduction by 30%
- Organic Traffic increase by 3x
- 4x increase in leads from organic traffic
- Fan base on Facebook has grown to an engaged community of over 140,000 fans.

Digital marketing is useful. However, you must first understand your target audience. In this way, you can fine-tune your online branding to create a consistent online presence that can help your brand in becoming recognizable.

# References

Behl, S. (2016). Digital Marketing for Real Estate: A complete Guide. Retrieved from https://www.digitalvidya.com/blog/real-estate-digital-marketing-guide/

Douglas, M. (2018). How Digital Marketing Will Change: Predictions for 2019 | DigitalMarketer. Retrieved from https://www.digitalmarketer.com/blog/digital-marketing-predictions-2019/

Golden, J. (2018). How Digital Marketing Will Transform Real Estate Industry In 2019. Retrieved from https://digitalagencynetwork.com/how-digital-marketing-will-transform-real-estate-industry-in-2019/

KPMG International. (2018). The road to opportunity An annual review of the real estate industry's journey into the digital age [Ebook] (1st ed., pp. 8-27). Retrieved from https://home.kpmg/content/dam/kpmg/uk/pdf/2018/09/kpmg-global-proptech-survey.pdf

LEE, C. (2018). Retrieved from https://www.lyfemarketing.com/blog/real-estate-digital-marketing/

Osumare. (2018). Marketing techniques that work wonders for Real Estate - Digital Marketing Blog - Osumare. Retrieved from http://osumare.com/blog/marketing-techniques-that-work-wonders-for-real-estate/

Raman, N. (2019). Real Estate | Digital Marketing For Real Estate | Social Beat. Retrieved from https://www.socialbeat.in/blog/digital-marketing-will-transform-real-estate-india/